this book belongs
to:

_____

Library of Congress Cataloging-in-Publication Data is available.
ISBN: 0-88396-627-1

Certain trademarks are used under license.

Manufactured in the United States of America.
Fifth Printing: 2003

Blue Mountain Arts®
P.O. Box 4549, Boulder, Colorado 80306

girls

rule

...a very special book
created especially for girls

Ashley Rice

Blue Mountain Press™
Boulder, Colorado

 # introduction:

My name is Penelope J. Miller, and I am the narrator of
this book. I'm here in the beginning to introduce the
book to you and to tell you "Hi." The pictures and poems
on these pages are messages from the heart, created
with the purpose of keeping girls posted on all the
possibilities that are out there and to remind them how
valued and talented they are. Some of the pages in this
book are also about the simple things in life. This makes
sense to me because when you are striving for great
things — achieving dreams and making your way in the
world — it is good to keep in mind the things that make
you happy. For me, Penelope J. Miller, those things include
reading books and sometimes eating chocolate. So that's
what this book is about: the life of girls (which is full of
color and fun things and chocolate), along with the
harder lessons we learn in life (which, though they are
hard, nevertheless help us achieve our dreams as well).
Yes, dreams take work — that's in this book, too —
but they also take dreaming. So whatever is going on
in your life right now, or wherever you are headed, I
hope that you have a great day and that all your
dreams come true.

your friend,

Penelope J.

A girl in the world is a wonderful thing

A girl in the world
is a wonderful thing.
She can do most anything
she puts her mind to.
She can write a book.
She can start a band.
She can become a doctor.
She can dream and plan.
She can handle adversity.
She can stand up tall.
And in all these things,
she is beautiful.
She is strong.
A girl in the world
is a wonderful thing.
She can do most anything
she puts her mind to.

As you go on in this world... always believe in your dreams. Keep looking forward to the future... to all you might be. Don't let old mistakes or misfortunes hold you down: learn from them, forgive yourself... or others... and move on. Do not be bothered or discouraged by adversity. Instead, meet it as a challenge. Be empowered by the courage it takes you to overcome obstacles. Learn things. Learn something new every day.

Be interested in others and what they might teach you. But do not look for yourself in the faces of others. Do not look for who you are in other people's approval. As far as who you are and who you will become goes — the answer is always within yourself. Believe in yourself. Follow your heart and your dreams. You... like everyone... will make mistakes. But so long as you are true to the strength within your own heart... you can never go wrong.

Always believe in your dreams.

 Always remember...

you are

loved

A Girl like You

She is a girl who changes minds, takes chances, turns heads, listens. She is the first to arrive, the last to leave, the first to lend a hand. She is a girl who remembers, pauses, makes an effort, laughs. She is unique, irreplaceable, real. That girl is... you!

In this world...

In this world,
there is only one
You.

You have your
very own ways.

You've got your own
walking shoes
in this world.

You are the
only one who
smiles and laughs
exactly as you do.

You are the
only one who lives
and thinks exactly
as you do.

You are your
very own you.

In this world,
there is only one
You.

You've got your
own dreams and
your ideas, too...

In this world,
there is only one
You.

Like a rainbow, you bring color to ordinary places. Like a sunset, you add brilliance. Like a river, you know the way. With the patience of the forests, you wait for your dreams to grow. And like the most special flower in the garden...

You grow
stronger and
more beautiful
every day.

Keep on growing

You are:

    1. talented

    2. real

    3. brave

    4. true to yourself

    5. loyal

and — most importantly:

    6. you never give up.

You Are a Lover of Words...
One Day, You Will
Write a Book

People turn to you because
you give voice to dreams, notice
little things, and make otherwise
impossible imaginings appear real.
You are a rare bird who thinks
the world is beautiful enough to
try to figure it out, who has the
courage to dive into your wild
mind and go swimming there.

You are someone who still believes in cloud watching, people watching, daydreaming, tomorrow, favorite colors, silver clouds, dandelions, and sorrow. Be sacred. Be cool. Be wild. Go far. Words do more than plant miracle seeds. With you writing them, they can change the world.

If you could read a book about your future, it would start out something like this →

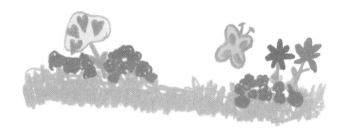

Many people speak of dreams
as fanciful things, like fairies
and charmed rings and lands
of enchantment. Others only
believe in faraway dreams,
such as stars or sea castles
with elf-like inhabitants.

There are day-dreamers and night-dreamers who dream up make-believe places. They use much imagination, and in that are dream-gifted. But the serious dreamers are those who catch dreams and bring them to life to show that when they were dreaming, they meant it.

How to be a rock star,
prize winner, teacher,
astrophysicist, novelist,
professional wrestler, actor,
painter, radio personality,
editor, filmmaker,
guitar player, columnist,
astronaut, singer, designer,
cartoonist, inventor,
architect, builder, producer,
writer, athlete, artist,
programmer, dancer,
technician, or stylist
in one step or less...

1. go for it.

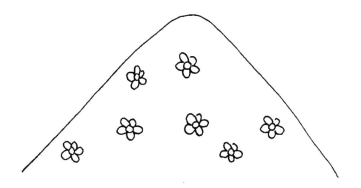

When the task at hand is a mountain
in front of you,
it may seem too hard to climb.
But you don't have to climb it
all at once —
just one step at a time.
Take one small step...
and one small step...
then another...
and you'll find...
the task at hand that was a mountain
in front of you...
is a mountain you have climbed.

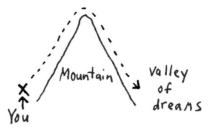

Imagine in your head the story of a very brave person who is capable, brilliant, and talented. In front of that person stands a very large mountain. She must climb this mountain in order to reach her goal — the valley of dreams which lies just on the other side. See that person approach the mountain? She is all determination. She has overcome similar obstacles before. Watch her now as she begins to climb. This is your story. It is you against that mountain now. Go find your valley of dreams.

You are strong!
You can do it!

You can do anything

If anyone tries to tell you that you can't work hard enough to face the task in front of you — show them that you're tough. If anyone tries to tell you that you are not that strong, don't listen to discouragement — know that you belong.

If anyone tries to tell you that
you can't sing your own song,
or make your way in the world...

prove them wrong.

Everyone gets an angel...

You can't always see them because
sometimes they are invisible.

Sometimes they are your pet
when he kisses you...

Sometimes they are a small treasure
you find...

an angel might even be your friend.

Those angels are quiet, but what they are
really saying is: "Pink clouds! A good day
is just around the corner."

 So if you begin to worry too much,
just remember...

Somewhere an angel
is looking out for you, too.

Sister-ness

Flowers today for sister-ness:

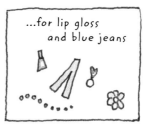

...for lip gloss and blue jeans

...for staying late to talk

...for road trips, soda, and daydreams

...for high school ways

...and college days

...and all the years in-between.

Flowers for the sisters we grow up with...

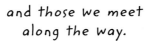

and those we meet along the way.

There Are Women Who
Changed My Life because
they were Mentors. There
Are Women Who Changed
My Life because they
were Friends. There
Are Women Who
Changed My
Life because
they were
Women.

you
are
an amazing
Woman

a few lessons
on life
from me (Penelope)...

on leaving:

when you are
getting ready
to leave a
place...

there are
a few things
you can do
to make yourself
feel less nervous...

pack a
teddy bear...

a few
happy
snapshots...

and your
favorite
book, to keep
you steady.

remember to
say goodbye
to everyone...

 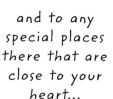

and to any
special places
there that are
close to your
heart...

(if you think you are
too old for a teddy bear,
you can pack something
else in place of it, but
the truth is: no one is
ever really too old for
a teddy bear.)

when you
go out there...

↖ world

↖ road
map

angel
↘

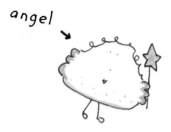

say your prayers...

remember:
take care
of yourself...

← clean
   laundry

go to sleep
at a decent hour...

↑ alarm
  clock

and eat your vegetables!

When things get
hard...

take a bath.

Taking a bath won't change
anything, but...

When you are in the bathtub,
you are not responsible for
anything — you are wet, for
example, so no one can ask you
to do anything... you can't do
homework in there, because your
papers will get wet... you can't
answer the phone... or read any
e-mail... or assignments... or
messages... or...

...maybe it should be
a long bath.

Some days...
  you just gotta
   forget it all...

...and dance.

This is your guardian
angel saying that
even if things
seem a little bit
crazy where you
are right now,
from up here
you look pretty
good... That
tangled mess that's got
you worried — it's just
a dark cloud...

and there's a rainbow
on the other side.

Don't think that it's such a terrible thing to get sad or down or to stop believing in sunshine for a while. Don't worry too much if you feel empty or lost or you can't make yourself want to smile.

Don't think that it's not okay to
want to sit a day out, or to be
scared or tired or blue. Everybody
gets sad sometimes. And crying
and hurting — just like laughing
and dreaming — are just things
that people do.

on dreams:

Oh, but for flying elephants and impossible staircases and weeping willows and talking walruses — where would we be? Oh, but for laughing alphabets and silly stories and mad rabbits dancing across the skies — what would get us through the nights? Oh, but for the will to read and dream and dance in yards and paint in between the lines — how could we say that something was not lost?...

Hold on to your dreams;
they are as precious as
laughter — they are
eternal, like stars.

on love:

The strange thing about love is that
it can make your heart beat faster, and
the strange thing about love is that it
can make you laugh and then cry. The
strange thing about love
is that it's uneven: in
this life, you may be
loved by someone
you don't love back,
and you may love
someone who
doesn't return
your love.

The strange thing about love is that it's always worth it, and the strange thing about love is that it is always there somewhere in your life. The strange thing about love is that you have to believe in it for it to be true, and the strange thing about love is that, even if it's a different story than you expected, somehow it all works out.

Love is strange, isn't it? But trust in it... and you will be all right.

on friendship:

Friendship is at the
heart, heart, heart
of all that matters

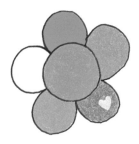

The love of a friend:
to see each other through
good days and bad days,
a hand to hold, a heart to
lend... someone you can
always count on to celebrate
and find rainbows with...
there is no
treasure more special.

Friends are angels sent
down to earth to make
good days and to help
us find our way.

your star

There is a star in the
sky... just for you.
That star will make sure
that your dreams
come true.

So in case you are
stumbling — don't get
too blue.
That star in the sky...
it believes in you.

And in case you were wondering...

I do, too.

(I believe in you and your star.)

you are a very
special star in this
world...

go on and shine
go on and shine
go on and
shine.

a place to
write your dreams

Place this book beside your bed near the pillow where you rest your head and know that the moon is shining bright, the stars keep watch over the night, and angels keep you safe; they listen to your dreams. Now close your eyes and rest your head; sleep quietly and peacefully in your own bed. Think of your favorite things, and have sweet dreams.